MISSION HILL
THROUGH TIME

Antnony M Sammarco

ANTHONY M. SAMMARCO
CONTEMPORARY PHOTOGRAPHS BY PETER B. KINGMAN

Peter B. Kingman

This book is in memory of Frank Norton

Opposite: Brigham Circle is the junction of Huntington Avenue, Tremont, Calumet and Francis Streets, and has long been a busy crossroads. Seen here in the late 1940s, hundreds of residents line the streets and the Brigham Circle park watching the Mission Church CYO Band parade through the neighborhood. In the distance is the Calumet Cafe, with stores along Huntington Avenue and the Brigham Circle Super Market on the right.

America Through Time is an imprint of Fonthill Media LLC
www.through-time.com
office@through-time.com

Published by Arcadia Publishing by arrangement with Fonthill Media LLC
For all general information, please contact Arcadia Publishing:
Telephone: 843-853-2070
Fax: 843-853-0044
E-mail: sales@arcadiapublishing.com
For customer service and orders:
Toll-Free 1-888-313-2665

www.arcadiapublishing.com

First published 2022

Copyright © Anthony M. Sammarco 2022

ISBN 978-1-63499-385-2

All rights reserved. No part of this publication may be reproduced, stored in a retrieval system or transmitted in any form or by any means, electronic, mechanical, photocopying, recording or otherwise, without prior permission in writing from Fonthill Media LLC

Typeset in Mrs Eaves XL Serif Narrow
Printed and bound in England

Contents

	Acknowledgments	4
	Introduction	5
1	Parker Hill	9
2	Mission Hill	21
3	Places of Worship	33
4	Roxbury Crossing	41
5	Hospitals	49
6	Schools	57
7	Along Huntington Avenue	69
8	Businesses	83
9	Urban Renewal	91

Acknowledgments

I wish to especially thank Peter Bryant Kingman for his wonderful contemporary photographs of the Mission Hill neighborhood of Boston. He has captured the essence of the vintage photographs and has made this book not just an interesting compilation of the houses, businesses, squares and streetscapes of this historic neighborhood of Boston, but a visually fascinating one as well.

We wish to extend our sincere thanks and deep appreciation to:

Heidi Adams; Laura Adams; Eric Alden, for his enthusiasm and research on Mission Hill; Michael Amaral; Joel Andreasen; The Basilica of Our Lady of Perpetual Help, Very Rev. Joseph Tizio, C.Ss.R, Rector; *Baystate Banner*, Melvin B. Miller, Publisher; Sher Beauliue; Boston Athenaeum, Sally Pierce and Catharina Slautterback; Boston City Archives; Boston Public Library, David Leonard; Kathryn Juel Brookins; Edward Burke; Mark Carrig; the late Hutchinson Cedmarco; Pasqualina Cedmarco; Cesidio "Joe" Cedrone; City of Boston, ISD, Brigid Kenny-White; Philip A. Clark; Philip E. Cleary; Edie Clifford; Colortek, Jackie Anderson; Congregational Library and Archives, William McCarthy and Zachary Bodnar; Maureen Connolly; Ruth Costello; Francis A. Countway Library of Medicine, Stephanie Krauss and Keith Pierce; Larry Cronin; Jean Di Giacomandrea; Digital Commonwealth; eBay; Patty Crossen Duane; Russell DuPont; Mary Ann English; Mary Fahey; Frances Feloni; Mary Fronk; Edward Gordon; Helen Hannon; Rev. Peter Johnston; George Kalchev, Fonthill Media; Historic New England, Lorna Condon; the late James Z. Kyprianos; Kena Longabaugh; the late Dr. Robert J. MacMillan; the Metropolitan Museum of Art; *Mission Hill Gazette*, Peter Shanley, Editor; Mission Grammar School, Elizabeth Looney, Principal; Mission Hill Main Streets; Marilyn R. Moody; New England Baptist Hospital; Frank Norton; Orleans Camera; the late Stephen Davies Paine; Susan W. Paine; Parker Hill Branch, Boston Public Library, Karen Gallagher; Robert Poulos; Steve Peluso; Mary Power; Lilian M.C. Randall; Roxbury Tenants of Harvard Association, Inc.; Anthony Salvucci; the late Dexter and Charlotte Tuttle Clapp Sammarco; Henry Scannell; Ron Scully; Deena Segal; Silverman Engineering Company; Spanish Church of God, Rev. Amaury Abreu; Ralph Spears; Alan Sutton, Fonthill Media; Jamie Sutton; Jack Sullivan; John Toner; Trinity Lutheran Church of Boston, Steve Vekasy, Pastor; Ken Turino and Chris Matthias; Archives and Special Collections, University of Massachusetts, Sammarco Collection; Lyn Wells; Wentworth Institute of Technology, Mark Thompson; Jerry Woodlock; Thomas Zaiko.

All photographs are from the Boston Public Library except as noted.

Introduction

Mission Hill is a neighborhood of Boston that is a part of Roxbury, Massachusetts. Settled in 1630, the area was once open land with farms and estates along the present-day Tremont and Heath Streets and Huntington Avenue. However, by the mid-nineteenth century, the city of Boston began not just topographical changes but expanded its accessibility from the one-time Neck, on Washington Street, that connected it to Roxbury. The area west of the Back Bay began to see accessibility that spurred development for both residential as well as commercial development.

Known as Parker Hill, in honor of John and Sarah Ruggles Parker, their farm had extensive orchards that survived into the early twentieth century. With small farms such as those of the Dudley, Davis and Curtis Families, there was also the estate of Colonel Francis Brinley, a wealthy merchant who inherited a large estate in Roxbury, upon which in 1723 he built an elaborate country house that he called *Datchet House*, named after his family seat in England, which today is the site of the Rectory to the Mission Church. However, because of the stone outcropping on Parker Hill, it began to be quarried for building material in the mid-nineteenth century. Along Tremont Street and up Parker Hill was a pudding stone quarry, a conglomerate stone that consists of distinctly rounded pebbles whose colors contrast sharply with the color of the finer-grained, often sandy, matrix, which became a popular building material for structures from the 1850 to 1910 period. These quarries would see the stone used for churches, houses and retaining walls not just in Roxbury but throughout the Boston area.

For the purposes of this book on *Mission Hill Through Time*, the neighborhood is bound by Columbus Avenue, Heath Street, South Huntington Avenue, the Riverway, Huntington Avenue and Ruggles Street and Tremont Street. This area was to see tremendous changes beginning in 1868 when the city of Boston annexed the city of Roxbury; by 1874, the city had also annexed Dorchester, Charlestown, Brighton and Allston, West Roxbury, Jamaica Plain and Roslindale. Accessibility from Huntington Avenue, and what is present-day Hemenway Street, would connect Mission Hill to Boylston Street in the Back Bay as did Tremont Street to the South End. However, it was the Redemptorists, the Congregation of the Most Holy Redeemer (who in 1870 built a modest wooden church on Tremont Street that was dedicated to Our Lady of Perpetual Help) who started the changes. Using the former *Datchet House*, which had once been the residence of General Henry Dearborn, and his son Henry A. S. Dearborn, the first mayor of Roxbury, the area evolved and became known as Mission Hill in honor of the church. Designed by William Schickel and Isaac Ditmars and built of locally quarried pudding stone, the church was consecrated in 1878. An icon of Our Lady of Perpetual Help was hung over the main altar in 1871, and not long after, miraculous cures were reported, attributed to the intercession of Our Lady. In 1874, the weekly practice of bestowing a blessing on the sick was formally established and Mission Church became a destination for those seeking a cure for ailments and infirmities, and between 1878 and 1884, over 300 cures were documented.

The area of Parker Hill, which had comfortable suburban villas built in the mid-nineteenth century (especially along Parker, Allegheny, Fisher and Hillside Streets and Parker Hill Avenue) had not just picturesque views, but at the crest of Parker Hill was once a reservoir, one of the retaining basins for the water system of the city of Boston. The Parker Hill Reservoir was built in 1874 and had a capacity of 7.2 million gallons. However, as it was at a much higher elevation than Fort Hill in Roxbury, the Parker Hill Reservoir was eventually discontinued and the nearby standpipe on Fort Hill replaced its use. In the 1830s, the Boston and Providence Railroad had a station at Roxbury Crossing and the ease of transportation allowed the development of Parker Hill for new residences, as did the "hourlies" started by Amos, Lewis and Hartford Morse, and later horse-drawn streetcars and then the electric streetcar after 1894, which connected the neighborhood to downtown Boston. With immigrants to Boston, and their children, they increased the population not just as a place of residence but also as employees of local businesses. There was ample employment in the mills along Stony Brook, which was a small river at the base of Parker Hill. With numerous breweries along the Stony Brook, German beer and ale began to be produced from its pure waters. The John R. Alley Brewery on Heath Street was built in 1886 and was known as the "Elbana" Brewery, for the Irish ale using the Greek word for Dublin. Others included Pfaff Brewery at Roxbury Crossing, the Rueter & Alley "Highland Spring" Brewery on Terrace Street (which, after it closed in 1919, was used as a warehouse by Oliver Ditson Company, the Boston music-publishing firm, and later as "The Pickle Factory"). The Andrew J. Houghton Brewery was on Halleck Street, the Continental Lager Beer Brewery on Longwood Avenue, the Park Brewery on Terrace Street and McCormick's Brewery on Conant Street. The American Brewing Company was on Heath Street and was one of the most elaborately designed breweries in Boston with a conical metal roof cap on the rounded bay and several clocks, which announced the shift hours to the brewery workers. The American Brewing Company was just one establishment of James W. Kenney, who also founded the Park Brewery on Terrace Street in 1882 and the Union Brewery on Terrace Street in 1893. Each of these breweries employed many hands and were successful until Prohibition. For non-alcoholic tastes, the Chelmsford Spring Company and the Nutro Beverage Company both produced ginger ale on Mission Hill, and to cleanse the body, the Nathan Soap Works.

As Sam Bass Warner said in his book *Streetcar Suburbs*:

> Throughout the three last decades of the [nineteenth] century the whole area served primarily as a "zone of emergence" for lower middle class immigrant families. Between 70 and 80 percent of its population was first and second generation foreign born.

The result was to be a housing boom on Mission Hill which attracted new residents with the housing stock being primarily three-deckers, apartment buildings and row houses, especially along Huntington Avenue and Tremont, Wigglesworth and Worthington Streets. The large landowners in this period were Franklin Dexter, Frederick Ames, Governor Eugene Noble Foss, Thomas Thacher, Warren Fisher and Lawrence Logan, who began to subdivide their land for residential development. As new streets were laid out by F. Gordon Dexter, it was interesting that some of them bore Native American names, such as Iroquois, Sachem, Calumet, Delaware, Pontiac, Pequot, Allegheny and Cherokee Streets. However, during this time, the establishment of what would become a major medical center in Boston was taking place; Longwood Avenue had the Harvard Medical School in the early twentieth century, but Parker Hill was to have the New England Baptist Hospital, opened in 1893 in the former Bond Mansion on Parker Hill Avenue by its founder Dr. Francis Fremont Whittier. In 1914, the Robert Breck Brigham Hospital was built on the site of the reservoir and on Parker Hill Avenue was the Cushing Hospital and the Women's Charity Hospital; Resthaven, a charitable nursing home, was on Fisher Avenue. The Peter Bent Brigham Hospital was built at Brigham Circle, the Collis Potter Huntington Memorial Hospital on Huntington Avenue and the Boston Psychopathic Hospital on Fenwood Road. The Boston Medical Library built Countway Library on Shattuck Street near Brigham Circle.

In 1940, urban renewal would change Mission Hill when the Mission Hill Housing Project was built on the site of what had been deemed slums. This was one of the first housing projects opened in the United States, and ironically, John J. Curley, the brother of Mayor James Michael Curley, was the first manager of the project. In 1958, the Boston Redevelopment Authority built high-rise apartments, called Mission Hill Main, near Huntington Avenue, which created not just additional housing but modern apartments. The Charlesbank Apartments, the Back Bay Manor (now known as City View at Longwood) and Franklin Square Apartments (now known as The Longwood) were to rival the building boom of the 1890s. Eventually, the medical and educational institutions increasingly encroached on the neighborhood and when Harvard University wished to build a large power generator, they reached a compromise with Mission Hill residents to build housing which led to the development of Mission Park on Huntington Avenue on the site of the House of the Good Shepard, which is owned and run by the "Roxbury Tenants of Harvard."

Today, Mission Hill is a thriving nexus of cultures, with residents as well as workers in the medical field making it a vibrant, engaging and busy neighborhood. Though Mission Hill is less than one square mile, it is a neighborhood in constant flux, with not just homeowners but renters, especially students, calling it home for a short period of time. What it lacks in area, Mission Hill makes up in character, maintaining a small neighborhood vibe while remaining one of Boston's most diverse areas. With a variety of housing, restaurants and pubs as well as accessibility, it also offers green spaces such as the Iroquois Woods, the Kevin W. Fitzgerald Park and the Back of the Hill Urban Wild, making it a small neighborhood that has not only evolved but embraced change over the last century in a big way.

The Basilica of Our Lady of Perpetual Help has long been an anchor not just on Mission Hill but in the city of Boston. Seen here in 1950, graduates of the Our Lady of Perpetual Help Mission Grammar School are seated in the church during a Mass to celebrate their graduation. Since 1889, under the direction of the School Sisters of Notre Dame, the school has provided academic achievement by the Sisters in their "ministry of education for the transformation of the world."

1

Parker Hill

Colonel Francis Brinley built *Datchet House* at the corner of Tremont and St. Alphonsus Streets in 1723. Seen in a portrait by John Smibert, Brinley was a graduate of Eton, having arrived in America in 1710. He would build his country seat in Roxbury which was "said to have been a slightly reduced version of the Brinley family H-plan house at Datchet, England," and cared for by a number of enslaved people. Brinley served as Surveyor General of his Majesty's Customs at Boston and was a member of the Vestry of King's Chapel. Seen through the window is a view of Boston in 1729. According to Stuart Feld: "Beyond the broad acreage called the 'Roxbury Flats' in the Burgiss map [of 1728,] the beacon that gave Beacon Hill its name is clearly visible at the left. The map further helps us to identify the two prominent structures in the middle distance as the 'Watch House' at the left and the 'Powder House' at the right." In the center is the Old South Meetinghouse and on the right is Christ Church in Boston. (Collection of the Metropolitan Museum of Art)

The Ebenezer Crafts House, a Second Period house with a massive coffered chimney, was built in 1709 on the Brookline Road (now Huntington Avenue) near Fenwood Street. It was on this farm that *Roxbury Russet* apples were first hybridized. They are the oldest named variety of apple in America with a green skin which is tinged a bronze, and overspread with a brownish-yellow russet. Later owned by Deacon Ebenezer Crafts, a cordwainer and well-known farmer, he owned about "thirteen acres of land lying on the northerly side of the road leading to Brookline, on which was located the house built by his father in 1709, together with twenty-seven acres of land lying close the road on the "Great Hill [Parker Hill]."

The Samuel Dudley House was built in the late eighteenth century on Tremont Street near Worthington Street. Seen in 1863, in the foreground is a rubble stone wall and a part of the pudding stone quarries that ascended Parker Hill; in the distance can be seen the marshes of what would be developed as the Back Bay Fens in the late 1880s. Samuel Dudley was a gentleman farmer who descended from Thomas Dudley, the second governor of Massachusetts Bay Colony and member of the first Board of Overseers for Harvard College and one of the most prominent men in Roxbury. In the distance is the Folsom's Oil Cloth Factory on Longwood Avenue.

The Benjamin Davis House was built on Washington Street (now known as Huntington Avenue) opposite Waitt Street. Benjamin Davis was a farmer whose land extended back towards the Riverway. He built his house in 1761, the year he married Sarah Winchester. Their son was Isaac Davis, who was to serve as a selectman and overseer of the poor, treasurer of the town of Roxbury from 1817 to 1845 and trustee f the Roxbury Latin School. The Davis Family lived in the house for generations until it was demolished in 1885. Today, the Farragut School and its playground is now on the site.

Datchet House was purchased by Robert Pierpont in 1773 and he created such a lavish seat that it was referred to as Pierpont's Castle. The Dearborn Family lived here until the 1831, after which it was purchased by Samuel S. Lewis, manager of the Cunard Steamship Line. In 1860, it opened as a summer boarding house and was known as the Franklin Gardens, a popular pleasure garden for food and drink. Sold in 1870, the house was extensively remodeled, and a new wood addition was built for the first place of worship of the Redemptorists, but it served as a "mission church," where only some Catholic rites were performed. It also served as a mission house, for Roman Catholic priests traveling to distant parts of Massachusetts, New England and Canada.

The Hayden House was built in 1828 at 231 Heath Street. A Greek Revival wood frame house, it had an impressive colonnade of Ionic columns that once overlooked terraced gardens that descended to the street. Judge Albert Fearing Hayden, whose father Isaac Hayden had an estate at Hayden and Fisher Streets on Parker Hill, was a judge in the Roxbury Municipal Court, who presided over the sentencing of people arrested during the May Day riots of 1919. This made him a target during the 1919 United States anarchist bombings when his house was bombed by the Italian anarchist followers of Luigi Galleani and nearly destroyed. Today, this is part of the Back of the Hill Community Development Corporation's twenty-two units of affordable housing on Wensley Street, Bickford Avenue and Fisher Avenue.

The Gray House was built in 1819 on Parker Street. A simple Greek Revival wood house, it was embellished by a three-sided colonnade of slender two-story columns. The pudding stone retaining wall, which is still intact today and extends from Delle Avenue to Allegheny Street, was built of locally quarried stone and provided a level grade for the property due to the steep incline of Parker Street. In the 1880s, the house and grounds were purchased by the daughters of Thomas and Caroline Billings Thacher and demolished, and the grounds were used as a garden. Today, this is now the schoolyard of the Fenway High School. (Author's Collection)

The Samuel Alds Way House, a Gothic Revival house with a crenelated cupola built in the 1850s from the designs of Andrew Jackson Downing from his book *Victorian Cottage Residences*, was a charming house built on Parker Street. Way was an entrepreneur, importing Holland Gin, which is said to have a smooth and very aromatic taste with malty flavors, and he became the largest importer of the gin in nineteenth- century Boston. His wealth allowed him to become a real estate investor and he built low-income rental houses on Way Street in Boston. Later, he founded the Bank of the Metropolis, a private bank on State Street in Boston, and the bank's connections "extended through the world with letters of credit being honored in every country and at every commercial center on the globe. As a financier, he has not his equal in State Street for genius and ability."

The Nahum Ward House was built at the corner of Ward and Parker Street. In 1828, Ward rented a small building on Ward Street in Roxbury and began business as a tallow chandler and soap-maker. By 1840, Ward was melting tallow, rendering the fat from cattle bones, and neatsfoot oil from cattle's shinbones and feet. The bone rendering factory in Roxbury grew tremendously and he contracted with the city of Boston to receive all the horse offal, averaging ten cords a day. Because of the stench in the rendering of bones, "Bony Ward" as he was popularly referred to, moved his horse-rendering facility in the 1850s to Spectacle Island in Boston Harbor where the "smell of the dump was so foul that in foggy weather ships could get their bearings simply by the stench emanating from the island." After his death in 1858, the business was known as the N. Ward Company, a glue manufacturing company. His house was a modest duplex house built in the 1830s and by the late nineteenth century was adjacent to Matthew J. Nolan's auto trimmer and harness shop, seen on the right and the Sewell and Day Cordage Company.

The Timothy Wright Hoxie House was built in 1854 as an Italianate design house near the crest of Parker Hill on Hillside Street. Hoxie was a successful commission merchant in Boston. The house, with impressive window trim, heavy bracketing and a prominent square-hipped roof tower, might have been designed by noted architect Luther Briggs, Jr. In the late nineteenth century, as land on Parker Hill was being developed, the Hoxie House was moved across the street next to the Greenleaf Sanborn House, a small cottage from the late 1840s that became the home of Reverend Andrew Stone, minister of the Park Street Church, and enlarged with an addition on the rear. The house was listed on the National Register of Historic Places in 1987.

The Ephraim Washington Bouvé House was built in 1850 at the corner of Parker and Allegheny Streets, adjacent to the family home of his wife, Adaline D. Gray, seen on the far right. Bouvé opened his printing business in 1832 and became a well-known engraver and cartographer and he chromolithographed sheet music covers in Boston, but he specialized in card engraving. According to family tradition, Bouvé was said to be "the fashionable engraver of his day, with a reputation for artistry." He had served as a member of the Roxbury City Council, and during the Civil War he was a member of the Roxbury Reserve Guard. He was commissioned as a justice of the peace for several terms and was a member of the Independent Order of Odd Fellows. Bouvé was typical of the aspiring middle-class individual moving to Parker Hill in the mid-nineteenth century. The house was moved across the street when Mission High School was built in 1926. (Author's Collection)

The Jacob Pfaff House is an impressive Italianate design house designed by Ferdinand Seiberlich, who was in partnership with J. N. Black, and built the house in 1865 at the corner of Parker Street and Delle Avenue. The Pfaff House was not only impressive but had corner quoining and a fashionable mansard roof. Pfaff, and his brother, Henry Pfaff, immigrated from Hochspeyer, Bavaria, in 1835, and in 1857 founded a well-known lager beer brewer which was at 1276 Columbus Avenue in Roxbury. The abundant and crystal-clear water from Stony Brook made Pfaff's one of the major brewers in the area. The H&J Pfaff Brewery imparted a little bit of old Germany that created a demand for the new German type Lager and Bock Beers and its slogan was "Best brewed because brewed best." On the left is the former Mission Church High School, now the Fenway High School on Allegheny Street, and on the right is a three-decker at 20 Delle Avenue.

2

MISSION HILL

The Mission Hill neighborhood evolved in the late nineteenth century as a close-knit community, often with generations of families living near one another. One place that was not just centrally located, but an important part of Mission Hill, is the Mission Hill Post No. 327 American Legion, which was built at the corner of Tremont and Wigglesworth Streets. The American Legion was chartered and incorporated by Congress in 1919 as a patriotic veterans' organization devoted to mutual helpfulness and is open to veterans as well as those in active duty. The hall was designed by Robert Charles Associates and built in 1962 of concrete, decorative concrete blocks and a brick facade and has long been an anchor, as well as a place of pride, on Tremont Street. Today the building is vacant and awaiting its future.

These elegant Queen Anne red brick and brownstone swell bay facade row houses are on Huntington Avenue between Wigglesworth Street and Brigham Circle. Designed by John H. Besarick, and built in 1888 by well-known builders Bosquet and Pepin, they created an urbane row of Mansard roof houses with impressive entryways with conical caps on the dormers. Albert Geiger, who developed this row of houses, was obviously extending the style of the houses of the Back Bay to Brigham Circle, though in a reduced size and scale. Today, the Mission Hill Triangle Architectural Conservation District preserves the late nineteenth century housing between Huntington Avenue and Tremont, Worthington and Smith Streets.

This row of houses was built on Tremont Street between Wigglesworth and Worthington Streets. It was anticipated that this area of Mission Hill would be developed with urbane brick or stone dwellings in the 1880s; these row houses were built by George D. Cox as early as 1872. During the late nineteenth century, these new row houses, and the nearby streets, used decorative elements derived from the Second Empire, Neo-Grec, Queen Anne, Panel Brick and Renaissance Revival architectural styles. Built with two stories and a dormered Mansard roof, they set the tone for the neighborhood. On the far left, an addition was added to the front of the row house on the left in 1962 for the Roxbury Council 123, Knights of Columbus.

Worthington Street, which extends from Huntington Avenue to Tremont Street, was land owned in the 1880s by various speculators including Winslow Warren, Moses Williams and Isabella Stewart Gardner. However, it was George D. Cox, a local builder, who was responsible for subdividing the land and laying out Wigglesworth and Worthington Streets. The row houses were built in the 1880s as red brick swell bay facade row houses with bracketed cornices and dormered Mansard roofs, similar in scale to those being built in the South End and Bay Village. John T. Broadhurst was to design the row of houses from 2 to 12 Worthington Street. Calixa Lavallee, composer of *O Canada*, the Canadian National Anthem, lived at 29 Worthington Street.

Wigglesworth Street, which paralleled Worthington Street, was developed by John F. Cornin, Robert W. Lord and Winslow Warren, who built two-story red brick row houses with three sided bays in the 1880s. John T. Broadhurst was the designer of rows at 1 toll Wigglesworth. 25 to 29 Wigglesworth were designed and built by McGowan and Galvin. Also during that year, 31 to 35 Wigglesworth and 26 and 28 Worthington were started by local builder Bartholomew J. Connally, designed by architect Charles A. Halstrom. 30 and 32 Worthington, designed by William Holmes and built by Mulligan and Gorham, were constructed the following year.

The Costello Family three-decker was designed by Samuel Rantin & Son and built in 1906 at the steep junction of Parker Hill Avenue and Calumet Street. John F. Costello was a prominent builder and developer, and this three-decker was not only dramatically sited at a junction between the two streets with side porches on the right, but it had Classical Revival details including swag panels above the first floor windows and shutters. Seen in 1908, the area of Parker Hill Avenue with the house of Frederick L. Ames on the upper left and Calumet Street and Parker Street in the foreground remained largely undeveloped in the early twentieth century.

22 Francis Street was designed by Patrick J. Cantwell and built in 1900 at the corner of Francis Street and Fernwood Road for Patrick Cannon. With a paneled first-floor entry and twin three-sided bays, it has a gable attic and flared aprons. Built on land that was once a part of the Ebenezer Francis Estate, it was subdivided in the 1890s by Jeremiah C. Spillane, a local real estate developer, and small house lots were laid out. Cantwell was a well-known architect, designing numerous houses in Roxbury and Brookline.

The lack of zoning in the early twentieth century on Mission Hill meant that were was a wide array of housing styles built between 1900 and 1940. Here 156, on the left, and 158 Calumet Street, represent a two-family built beside a three-decker. 156 Calumet Street was built in 1898 as a two-family Colonial Revival design with a recessed Gambrel roof with a shorn cap. The tri-part Palladian window and decorative railings are attractive features. 158 Calumet Street was designed by Samuel Rantin & Son and built in 1898. Straightforward in design, it has a rounded and three-sided bay with interesting tung and groove wood panels on the facade.

An interesting streetscape on Mission Hill is this trio of buildings at 96-98, on the left, and 100 and 102 Calumet Street. 96-98 Calumet Street, along with 92-94 to the far left, were designed by John O'Brien, a local builder, and built in 1898. Built of buff brick with granite trim, lintels and a rusticated arched doorway surround these two duplexes with their capped rounded bays. 100 Calumet Street was designed by Samuel Rantin and Son and built in 1898 as a Colonial Revival three-decker, a Palladian window in the attic, facade paneling on a rounded and three-sided bay and a bracketed cornice. 102 Calumet Street was designed by R. A. Watson and built in 1897 as a two-family Colonial Revival house with a marvelous classical string course of trailing vines and shells at the base of the gable attic.

36 and 38 Cherokee Street are two three-deckers that were designed by Samuel Rantin and Son, but separated by eight years—the left in 1896 and the right in 1904. These were speculative houses built by John M. Kelley, a builder from Roslindale, with architectural similarities such as the attic gables and bracketed cornice, but each has distinctive bays, rounded, pointed and three-sided bays, all of which added an element of uniqueness for the three-decker design.

St. Alphonsus Street ascends Parker Hill from Tremont Street and these three-deckers have a wonderful view of the twin spires of the Basilica. Appletree Pond was once located here and was filled in. St. Alphonsus and Hillside Streets were laid out. 170, on the left, and 172 St. Alphonsus Street, are wood three-deckers with frontal attic gables which were built for Michael Niland in 1902 and Catherine Niland in 1900 respectively, and designed by Samuel Rantin and Son as high-style Colonial Revival three-deckers. 174 St. Alphonsus Street on the right was designed by Samuel Rantin and built in 1898 for Catherine Niland as a brick three-decker with a dormered pitch roof. Samuel Rantin designed numerous houses on Mission Hill and Parker Hill during his architectural career.

30 Francis Street, at the corner of St. Albans (originally Crowley) Street, is an impressive red brick and brownstone three-decker, with terra cotta surrounds on the arched facade windows and copper rounded and octagonal bays and bracketed cornice. Designed by Timothy J. Desmond and built in 1900 for Daniel Crowley, it was built with large apartments. On the right is 32 Francis Street, a wood Classical Revival three-decker designed by Fred N. Mahony and built in 1898. Notice the double octagonal bays on the facade, a pedimented roof and the plaster swag detailing on the third floor. Many of the three-deckers on Francis Street were designed by architects such as Fred N. Mahoney, Patrick J. Cantwell, Samuel Rantin, Timothy J. Desmond, John T. O'Neil and Cornelius Russell.

3

PLACES OF WORSHIP

The golden icon of Our Lady of Perpetual Help has long been associated with the Redemptorists who founded the Mission Church in Roxbury in the nineteenth century. The icon originated from the Keras Kardiotissas Monastery in Crete and is today enshrined in the **Church of Saint Alphonsus** Liguori on the Esquiline Hill in Rome and has been revered by the Redemptorists since 1865. The Greek inscriptions on the icon read ΜΡ-ΘΥ (Μήτηρ Θεοῦ, *Mother of God*), ΟΑΜ (Ὁ Ἀρχάγγελος Μιχαήλ, *Michael the Archangel*), ΟΑΓ (Ὁ Ἀρχάγγελος Γαβριήλ, *Gabriel the Archangel*) and IC-XC (Ἰησοῦς Χριστός, *Jesus Christ*), respectively. In 1878, the Basilica of Our Lady of Perpetual Help on Mission Hill obtained a certified copy of the icon being the first church in the United States to do so.

The Highland Congregational Church was built in 1871 on Parker Street. Having previously worshiped in a small chapel on Parker Street, their new church was a result of Parker Hill being developed as a residential neighborhood with an increased population near Roxbury Crossing. On the left is the Samuel Alds Way House, a Gothic Revival house built in the 1850s from the designs of Andrew Jackson Downing whose book *Victorian Cottage Residences* was to introduce to Victorian Boston the tasteful, efficient cottage residence including Gothic Revival, Bracketed, Italianate, and Rustic designs. On the right is the Benjamin F. Bean House, an Italianate design duplex house on Oscar Street. (Courtesy of the Congregational Library and Archives in Boston, Massachusetts)

The Highland Congregational Church was designed by Benjamin Henry Brooks and Roger Drury and built in 1871 on Parker Street. The wood Gothic Revival church had a center entrance with three lancet windows above, a trefoil window and an asymmetrical spire that at that time was the highest point on Parker Hill. Oscar Street, on the upper right, and on the far right the corner of the Pfaff House at Delle Avenue, show an area that was developed in the mid-nineteenth century by affluent residents. Today, this is the Iglisia de Dios Church. (Courtesy of the Congregational Library and Archives in Boston, Massachusetts)

The Eliot Mission Society Chapel and Sunday School, under the auspices of the Eliot Church in Roxbury, built this Italianate design wood chapel in 1857 as a Sunday School and was known as Day's Chapel, in honor of Moses Day, the school superintendent. In 1871, the building was bought by the German Evangelical Lutheran Trinity Church as their first place of worship on Parker Hill, and in 1872, a second floor was added as it was not just a place of worship, but used as a parochial school and a social hall. Later known as Luther Chapel, in honor of Martin Luther, it is now the ABCD Parker Hill Fenway Head Start. (Courtesy of the Congregational Library and Archives in Boston, Massachusetts)

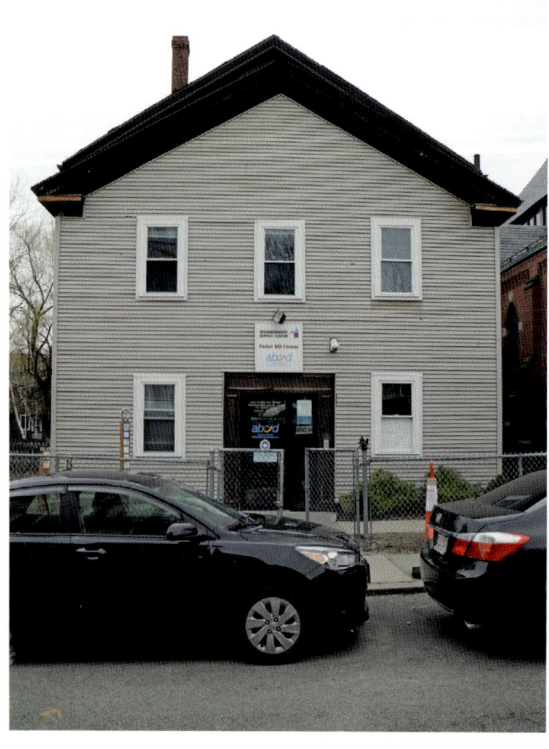

The German Evangelical Lutheran Trinity Church was founded in 1871 and the church was designed by Gilbert and Butler and Jacob Luippold and built in 1892 at Parker and Gore Streets. On the left is Luther Hall, the original place of worship as early as 1871 when the Reverend Adolph Biewend began his ministry. A red brick and sandstone Gothic Revival church with lancet doorways surmounted by three lancet windows, it had several memorial windows donated by early church members that included the Doerr, Gebhardt, Haffenreffer, Herthel, Mock, Sturm, Burkhardt and Ganser Families. It was later used as the New Life Presbyterian Church and the Gloucester Memorial Presbyterian Church, named for former slave, John Gloucester, who founded the first Black Presbyterian Church in the United States. Today this is the ABCD Parker Hill Fenway Head Start. (Courtesy of Trinity Lutheran Church, West Roxbury)

The Basilica of Our Lady of Perpetual Help was designed by William Schickel and Isaac Ditmars and built in 1878 in the Romanesque style. It was built of locally quarried pudding stone and Quincy granite at the crest of Tremont Street in Roxbury. The design was as urbane as it was impressive as Schickel had begun his career with Richard Morris Hunt, and Ditmars trained with John Miller and they were best known for their ecclesiastical work. Seen here in 1879, it was an imposing church surmounted by an octagonal lantern in a then largely undeveloped section of Roxbury. In 1883, the Archdiocese of Boston bestowed the status of a full parish church on Our Lady of Perpetual Help. On the far left is the Datchet House, occupied by the Dearborn Family from 1809 to 1831, a long low building that was later remodeled in 1870 by the firm of Quick & Klein of Philadelphia as the first place of worship of the Redemptorists. (Author's Collection)

The Blessing of the Bells at Mission Church took place on July 3, 1910. The staging was in place as the spires surmounting the original church neared completion. The western tower houses twelve bells that were named in honor of Our Lady of Perpetual Help, St. Joseph, St. Patrick, St. Alphonsus, St. Clement Hofbauer, St. John, St. Francis Xavier, St. Gerard Majella, St. Michael, St. Gabriel, St. Florian and St. Cecilia. Thousands of people, not just members of the congregation but interested Bostonians, came to witness this historic occasion. On the left is the flag draped Rectory of the Redemptorists. The church is considered not just the symbol of the Mission Hill neighborhood, to which it gives its name, but as a place of known miracles.

The twin spires of the Mission Church were designed by Franz Joseph Untersee, who also designed the Rectory, built in 1903 with paneled brick and limestone pilasters on the facade. The Munich Style stained-glass windows in the nave were made by Franz Xavier Zettler, his company having been appointed in 1882 by King Ludwig II as the Royal Bavarian Art Institute for Stained Glass in Munich, Germany; the windows in the shrine were made by Joseph Gabriel Mayer, Zettler's father-in-law, also from Munich; the original marble altar was designed by Father Louis Dold. The church was elevated to a minor basilica status in 1954 by Pope Pius XII and thereby received papal privileges; the church is entitled to a coat of arms, a small tower with a bell to carry during processions, and an umbrellina. Mission Church is one of only fifty-three churches designated a minor basilica in the United States.

4

ROXBURY CROSSING

Roxbury Crossing, the intersection of Tremont Street and Columbus Avenue, became a station of the Boston and Providence Railroad that was built to connect Boston and Providence, Rhode Island. This station was opened in 1845 and was a major reason that residential development on Parker Hill took place in the nineteenth century. The Roxbury Crossing Station, seen on the right, was reopened in 1897 when the Old Colony Railroad (which had acquired the Boston and Providence in 1888, and was itself acquired in 1893 by the New York, New Haven and Hartford Railroad) raised the railroad tracks from grade level through Roxbury and Jamaica Plain and built a spanned archway that allowed traffic to pass under it to Mission Hill. Today, the Ruggles MBTA Station services this area. On the left is the rear of the Highland Congregational Church on Parker Street.

The Romanesque Revival Roxbury Crossing Station was raised from grade level and a new ground floor structure was built under it in 1897 of hammered granite, allowing a thirteen foot raised track and sheltered waiting platform. The streetcar in the foreground provided transportation along Columbus Avenue to Egleston Station on the Boston Elevated Railway, fondly known as the El. Because of the competition of the Elevated Railway, the Roxbury Crossing Station was closed in 1940 due to a lack of passengers, as it was easier to take a streetcar or the El into Boston. Today there is a Roxbury Crossing station on the Orange Line of the MBTA.

Seen in 1934, the two high tracks of the New York, New Haven and Hartford Railroad were carried on an arched trestle over Tremont Street. After the bridge masonry had been completed and the bridge material received, the bridge for the westerly tracks at Roxbury driveway was erected in the place for the easterly tracks and the ballast and ties put on, and one Sunday night, after the last train had passed, the two westerly tracks over the driveway were taken up, the trestle removed, the new bridge slid over into its proper position and the tracks connected again before the first morning train was due. The bridge for the easterly tracks was then erected and the roadway underneath surfaced. The maze of streetcar tracks seen in the foreground showed how busy the area was in the 1930s with trains, streetcars, automobiles and pedestrians.

Streetcar 5712 emerges from under the bridge from Tremont Street. The policeman's stand on the right, shielded with a large black umbrella from the summer sun, had a policeman from Station 10, whose headquarters were just across the street, directing traffic. As John Goode said of his policeman father: "Even when my father was directing traffic in the late forties and early fifties [the stand] was gone and lights had been installed. They'd be switched to a flashing yellow during rush hour and guys like my father would direct traffic by hand. He didn't need to blow a whistle, either. He had a loud, strong whistle that he could do naturally." The tall building on the right was originally the Thomson-Crooker Shoe Company and later was the Trimount Clothing Company at 18 Station Street. Morris Shapiro, president of Trimount, under the name *Clipper Craft*, promoted the Ivy League Look. *Clipper Craft* was a brand that explicitly touted its Ivy League authenticity in advertisements in mainstream magazines. The company also offered "The Racer" brand of men's overcoats and suits, and in the 1960s, their "Mr. Cool" suit was said to be the world's lightest suit. The site is today a parking lot.

Roxbury Crossing, seen from Columbus Avenue (originally known as Pynchon Street) towards Tremont Street with Texas Street on the left, has the Plaza Theatre where Frances Feloni recalled there were "Lots of great movies and so many Saturday afternoon kids shows. Two movies, newsreel, cartoons, and coming attractions. You really got your money's worth at 25 cents." To the right is the Emmes Building and further down was a busy intersection, but in the 1960s, there was a plan to extend Interstate 95 into Boston along the NY, NH&H Railroad right-of-way, and hundreds of houses and businesses were taken by eminent domain and demolished. Residents protested this wholesale urban renewal, and the project was eventually halted in 1969, after the area had already become a barren wasteland.

The Plaza Theatre was at the corner of Columbus Avenue and Texas Street. Built as the Superb Theatre in 1917, it was renamed the Eliot Theatre in 1921. During the early years it not only showed silent films but also had amateur night, and according to Fred Allen, he played at this theater twice, once at an "Amateur Night" show and later as a small-time professional comedian. Eventually known as the Criterion Theatre, it became the Plaza Theatre in 1941, although it became known locally as the "Spit Box" due to the cheeky teenagers seated in the balcony. Seen in the mid-1940s, the marquee advertises *Buck Privates* with Abbott and Costello, the first service comedy based on the peacetime draft of 1940. In the center are shops including Robinson's Hardware Store, Kennedy's Butter and Egg, Weinstein's, Woolworth's, Hunt Drug Store, Police Station 10 and Robie's Rent-A-Car, operated by Richard Robie, who was a pioneer in the car rental business and acquired Avis Corp. from Warren Avis in 1954.

Looking east from Roxbury Crossing is Columbus Avenue on the left and Tremont Street on the right, which leads to the South End. The wide expanse of Roxbury Crossing had mostly small shops and stores, including the the New Haven Cafeteria on the left, and the Famous Twin Donought Shop in the center with the billboard advertising Cott Ginger Ale. Do you remember the slogan "It's Cott to be good?" On the right is the Plaza Theatre, the Emmes Building and a Hunt Rexall Drug Store, with Pynchon Street on the far right. After the 1960s, the street configuration was radically changed and at the junction of Tremont Street and Malcolm X Boulevard, the east remained Tremont Street and the west Columbus Avenue.

In 1894, the State legislature established the Boston Board of Street Commissioners, which extended streets to the new neighborhoods of Boston. Columbus Avenue was extended from the South End to Franklin Park at Egleston Square as an impressive boulevard that also had electric streetcar tracks. Completed in 1895, the new Columbus Avenue was built concurrently with the railroad viaduct; seen here in the 1950s, this is near the intersection of Columbus Avenue and Heath and Centre Streets. Seen on the right, the Cochituate Standpipe, designed by architect Nathaniel J. Bradlee and built in 1869 on Fort Hill, modernized Roxbury's water system. Other than the Standpipe and housing surrounding it on the upper right, this area in the foreground was obliterated in the late 1960s.

5

HOSPITALS

The New England Baptist Hospital was founded in 1893 as the Boston Baptist Hospital. The hospital purchased the Francis A. Bond house on the crest of Parker Hill Avenue, where it was thought that the fresh air provided an escape from the noise and congestion of the city for patients who might benefit from long-term rest and relaxation. Today, the hospital specializes in a full range of services in orthopedics and rheumatology, occupational medicine and sports medicine, foot and ankle care, joint replacement and spinal care and is the official hospital of the Boston Celtics. In 2017, the New England Baptist Hospital joined with Lahey Health and Beth Israel Deaconess Medical Center.

The Cushing Hospital was founded in 1893 by Dr. Ernest Watson Cushing as a private hospital with twenty-two beds in a pleasant shingle-style building on Parker Hill Avenue. Here he devoted himself exclusively to surgery and the diseases of women, and he opened a training school for nurses. Dr. Cushing's daughter, Dr. Olga Cushing Leary, said, "The hospital was of great interest to him in his later life and has expanded into a general surgical and maternity hospital with a very efficient training school." With its elevated location on Parker Hill, many of the private rooms opened onto the veranda by long windows, through which a bed or couch can be passed, so that patients who required systematic open-air treatment by night and day could receive particular attention under very advantageous circumstances.

The Women's Charity Club Hospital was opened in 1892 on Parker Hill Avenue through efforts of the Women's Charity Club, founded by Mrs. Micah Dyer, which conceived the idea of starting a free hospital for respectable women without means but in need of important surgical operations. Through fairs, musicals, tableaux vivants, literary readings and a sewing circle, members of the club raised necessary funds to sustain the W.C.C., as it was locally known, which was a benevolent, thirty-bed hospital for destitute women. As a gynecological and surgical hospital, it was under the direction of Dr. Edith M. Brooks, and later, Dr. Florence W. Duckening.

The Peter Bent Brigham Hospital was designed by Codman & Espadrille and built in 1913 facing Brigham Circle, the junction of Huntington Avenue and Francis Street on the former Ebenezer Francis Estate. Peter Bent Brigham was a self-made man who owned a restaurant on the corner of Hanover and Court Streets in Boston, Massachusetts, which he operated until it was sold in 1869. He is best known as a philanthropist for his initial endowment of Peter Bent Brigham Hospital, which was to be used to establish a hospital "for the care of sick persons in indigent circumstances." Just around the corner was the Commonwealth of Massachusetts Observational Hospital on Fernwood Road.

The Robert Breck Brigham Hospital was designed by Shepley Rutan & Coolidge as a brick Georgian Colonial Revival hospital with Ionic columns that initially had beds for fifteen patients. Brigham had endowed the hospital, which was established for infectious disease, in 1900. This was one of the few chronic disease hospitals in the country and became well known for the treatment of arthritis and rheumatic disease, and for its work in reconstructive orthopedic surgery.

The Collis Potter Huntington Memorial Hospital, later known as the Harvard School of Public Health, was designed by Shepley, Rutan and Coolidge and built in 1912 at the corner of Huntington Avenue and Shattuck Street. Established for the care of cancer patients, and research into the disease, no other organization for cancer research was said to be more "favorably situated, and it is equally true that the field of tumor investigation is of such breadth and importance to the public health that it calls for liberal support." Built under the direction of the Harvard Cancer Commission, it was named for Huntington, who was an American industrialist, railroad magnate and investor in the Central Pacific Railroad's expansion across the West. Huntington became president of the Southern Pacific–Central Pacific rail system in 1890 and thus controlled a vast empire of rail lines in California until his death in 1900.

The Countway Library was designed by Hugh Stubbins and Associates and dedicated in 1965 at 10 Stattuck Street. It was named for Francis A. Countway, president of Lever Brothers. Established in 1875 as the Boston Medical Library, it moved from the Fenway to Mission Hill in 1960 when the Boston Medical Library and the Harvard Medical Library combined their collections. The mission of the Countway Library is "to cultivate and advance education, research, scholarship and professional growth in the health and biomedical sciences by facilitating access to scholarly information and knowledge, preserving a historical record, and creating a stimulating and synergistic setting for intellectual growth."

The Boston Psychopathic Hospital was designed by Kendall, Taylor and Company and built in 1912 at 74 Fenwood Road, near Brigham Circle. The Late Gothic Revival design hospital was built of red brick with limestone string courses and was originally known as the Psychopathic Ward of Boston State Hospital. Dr. Elmer E. Southard was the first director of the hospital, which was among the first mental health hospitals, versus asylums, in Massachusetts. It had an inpatient unit and outpatient care that included a speech clinic that primarily treated patients who stuttered. Southard was ably assisted by Dr. L. Vernon Briggs, a longtime advocate for mental health. In 1920, it was separated from Boston State Hospital, which was located on the Austin Farm in Mattapan, and officially renamed the Boston Psychopathic Hospital. It was known for an approach centered on mental treatment rather than custodial care. In the late 1960s, the name was again changed to the Massachusetts Mental Health Center. Though the hospital was placed on the National Register of Historic Places, it was closed in 2010 and demolished in 2011. Today, the Massachusetts Mental Health Center continues to operate at 75 Fenwood Road.

6

SCHOOLS

Wentworth Institute of Technology was founded in 1904 through the benevolence of Arioch Wentworth, whose bequest established an industrial school for students to learn skills that involved working with their hands in a variety of trades. Incorporated the following year, the school was established "to furnish education in the mechanical arts." In 1911, Wentworth opened, and as their mission states, it "provides a project-based education in engineering, technology, design and management that integrates classroom, laboratory, studio, and experiential learning resulting in a career-ready, skilled professional and engaged citizen." Seen in 1918 at Camp Wentworth, the 101st Regiment United States Engineers are in training with tents set up on the land between Parker Street and Huntington Avenue. Wentworth became a degree-granting institution in 1957 and awarded its first baccalaureate-level degrees in 1970. In 2017, the school received approval for university status from the Massachusetts Department of Higher Education.

The Sisters' Convent of Our Lady of Perpetual Help was designed by Henry Burns and is at the corner of St. Alphonsus and Smith Street. To the left is the impressive Our Lady of Perpetual Help Grammar School, which was also designed by Henry Burns and built in 1889 with a pudding stone ground-floor and red brick and limestone Romanesque Revival school. Today, this is the Harvard T. H. Chan School of Public Health. To the far left is St. Alphonsus Hall, which was designed by architect Franz Joseph Untersee, and built in the Romanesque Revival style of Roxbury pudding stone. It was a part of the Basilica complex. St. Alphonsus Hall also boasted a library, a recreation room and a two-lane bowling alley. The play *Pilate's Daughter* was often performed during the Easter season, and was touted as America's oldest passion play by the Redemptorists.

The Martin School was designed by Arthur H. Vinal, city architect of Boston from 1884 to 1887, and built in 1885. Named for Augustus Pearl Martin, mayor of Boston in 1884, his legacy to the city was "a plain, practical, resolute, and honest government." Martin served as an artillery officer during the Civil War, was the leader of the state's Military Order of the Loyal Legion of the United States and served as commander of the Ancient and Honorable Artillery Company in 1878. Ever the consummate politician, he also served as chairman of the Board of Police and as city water commissioner. He was a very well-rounded politician.

The Comins School was built in 1854 at the corner of Terrace and Tremont Streets. The four-story school was named for Linus Bacon Comins, a patent leather manufacturer, who served as mayor of Roxbury in 1854 and was a member of the United States House of Representatives from Massachusetts from 1855 to 1859. The building was later repurposed as the Mission Church Press Building, where *The Pilot* newspaper, numerous books and the weekly bulletin of the Mission Church were printed. Interestingly, the Worcester Turnpike mile marker slate stone was set in the stone and granite retaining wall in front of the Comins School and is inscribed "To Boston Line 1 M 1810," which was an important way to gauge travel in the early nineteenth century. Today, this is the site of the Roxbury Crossing Condominiums, with the stone and granite retaining wall still in place.

The Charles Bulfinch School, named for the architect of Federal Boston and of the Massachusetts State House, was designed by Charles R. Greco and built in 1911 cantilevered to the corner of Parker and Fisher Streets. The red brick Tapestry Brick style school was a unique W-shaped schoolhouse on a square lot, set high on the corner. In 1910, the City of Boston took land originally owned by Peter Parker for the school, as the number of school age children in the neighborhood had increased tremendously. Today, the school was repurposed by Warren Freedenfeld & Associates as the Bulfinch Apartments.

David G. Farragut Elementary School was designed by Edmund March Wheelwright of Wheelwright and Haven and built in 1904 as a brick and limestone school at the corner of Huntington Avenue and Fenwood Road. The school was named for Admiral David G. Farragut, the first admiral in the United States Navy. He is remembered for his order at the Battle of Mobile Bay usually paraphrased as "*Damn the torpedoes, full speed ahead*" in true United States Navy tradition. During the Civil War he captured New Orleans in 1862 and commanded the Union Navy at Port Hudson and Mobile Bay attacks. Just to the left can be seen the locally famous bar the Hitching Post. The school was closed in 2011 and is today the Edward M. Kennedy Academy for Health Careers, for students who express an interest in the health professions.

The Ira Allen School was designed by Wilson and Webber and built 1901 at the corner of Parker and Edgar Streets. The school was named for Dr. Ira Allen who served as chairman of the Boston School Committee from 1868 to 1875. The school was purchased by Wentworth Institute in 1991, and now houses the Applied Mathematics and Sciences Department, faculty offices, laboratories, and classrooms. On the far left is the Annunciation Greek Orthodox Cathedral of New England, designed by Hachadoor S. Demoorjian and built in 1923 at the corner of Ruggles Street.

Boston Industrial School for Boys, later referred to as Trade High School, was designed by James E. McLaughlin and built in 1917 the corner of Parker and Archibald Streets. Trade schools, sometimes referred to as vocational schools, offer skills-based educational programs that prepared students for occupations in the trades such as plumbing, welding, electricity, woodworking and automotive, and this school even boasted an aviation course. Boston Trade stressed hands-on training over academics, and they had a well-regarded automotive repair program. The school closed 1978 and was merged into Madison Park High School in Roxbury.

Girl's Latin School and the Normal School were designed by Peabody and Stearns, Maginnins, Walsh and Sullivan and Coolidge and Carlson and built in 1907 on Huntington Avenue. The Beaux Arts design with red brick with terra cotta and limestone trim created a formal facade for the two schools. Later, these two schools were used by the Massachusetts College of Art and the Roxbury Community College. Girl's Latin School was founded in 1878 and was the first college preparatory high school for girls in the United States, and today is known as Boston Latin Academy. In 1872, the Boston Normal School separated from Girls' High School and became an independent institution, as an institution to train high school graduates to be teachers by educating them in the norms of teaching and curriculum. In 1924, the Normal School became the Teachers College of the City of Boston. In 1983, the Massachusetts College of Art took over the Girls' Latin School and Normal School buildings and began a program of renovation and expansion.

The Maurice J. Tobin School was designed by David B. Coletti of the Coletti Brothers Architectural Firm and built in 1959 at 40 Smith Street. The school was named in honor of Tobin, a native of Mission Hill, who served as Mayor of Boston (1938-45), Governor of Massachusetts (1945-47), and U. S. Secretary of Labor in the Truman Administration (1948-53.) In 1967, the Mystic River Bridge was renamed the Maurice J. Tobin Memorial Bridge. Today, the Tobin School is an extended service K-8 magnet school that engages school staff, families and community partnerships to help students' social and emotional well-being as well as their academic success. Warner Larson Landscape Architects created the Ida B. Graves Memorial Yard, which includes a community garden, stage and pavilion with lawn gathering space, outdoor dining with café and picnic tables and a shady outdoor classroom adjacent to the Tobin School.

The Mission Church High School was designed by Franz Joseph Untersee and built in 1926 on Allegheny Street. Under the direction of the Xaverian Brothers, the high school was opened in 1926. A Xaverian education at Mission High School was deeply rooted in the tradition, mission and the values of the Xaverian Brothers; the core values of humility, trust, zeal, compassion and simplicity was woven into not just education, but in all aspects of life. After six decades of education, Mission Church High School was closed due to declining enrollment at the end of the school year in 1992. The building was sold to the Boston Public School system and became the New Mission High School, which later moved to Hyde Park and is today the award-winning pilot school, the Fenway High School.

The House of the Good Shepherd was established in 1867 and located at 841 Huntington Avenue, opposite Parker Hill Avenue in Roxbury, Massachusetts. Founded by Bishop Williams of Boston, its object was "to provide a refuge for the reformation of fallen women and girls." Managed by the Sisters of the Good Shepherd, it had provision for 150 girls and women, of all creeds and denominations, with shelter, food and employment and instruction in religion and good morals, as well as reading and writing. Today, the property has been developed as Mission Park with mixed high-rise and townhouses by Roxbury Tenants of Harvard Association, Inc., a non-profit housing and human service organization that was founded by residents of the neighborhood in 1969. A portion of the gates and brick wall along Huntington Avenue still survives. (Author's Collection)

7

ALONG HUNTINGTON AVENUE

The Boston Fire Department Engine 37, Ladder 26 was designed by Krokyn, Brown and Rosenstein and built in 1933 at Huntington Avenue and Ruggles Street; the fire house is a three-bay brick and stone Classical Revival design with Doric pilasters and corner quoining. Engine 37 is said to be one of the busiest engine companies in the city on an annual basis. The engine company responds to approximately 3,900 incidents per year and Ladder 26 is also a very busy company, responding to approximately 3,800 incidents per year. To the right are two brick and stone apartment buildings designed by Silverman, Brown and Haven and built in 1924; today they are Edwards Hall and Rodgers Hall of Wentworth Institute. Notice the Charlesbank Cooperative apartment building in the distance and on the right the Francois-Xavier Bagnoud Building of the Harvard T. H. Chan School of Public Health.

Sparr's Drug Store was at the corner of Huntington and Longwood Avenues and founded by Joseph Sparr in 1933. His son, Arthur Sparr, a graduate of the Massachusetts College of Pharmacy, which was across the street, continued his father's store, which not only filled prescriptions and sold medical equipment, but was one of Boston's old-time drug store lunch counters with a soda fountain that served the best Raspberry Lime Rickies, as well as breakfast and lunch. Coffee sustained many residents and those working in the medical institutions on Longwood Avenue. The pharmacy closed in 2002, and the building was sold to the Harvard Medical School. On the left is the *Ormonde* Apartment Building, built in 1914, that was designed by Edwin K. Blaikie of Blaikie and Blaikie Architects, which specialized in commercial buildings and multi-family dwellings. On the right are the *Carlton*, designed by William Holmes and built in 1892, and *West Court*, designed by John Holmes and built in 1900, both apartment buildings.

Looking east on Huntington Avenue, on the right is the *Harvard* Apartment building and just beyond a Howard Johnson's Restaurant at the corner of St. Alphonsus Street with a neon sign in front. Howard Johnson created an orange-roofed empire of restaurants that stretched from Maine to Florida and from the East Coast to the West Coast. Popularly known as the "Father of the Franchise Industry," Johnson and his numerous franchise restaurants delivered good food and ice cream at reasonable prices that brought appreciative customers back for more. The attractive white Colonial Revival restaurants, with eye-catching orange porcelain tile roofs, illuminated cupolas, and sea blue shutters, were described in *Reader's Digest* in 1949 as the epitome of "eating places that look like New England town meeting houses dressed up for Sunday." (Courtesy of Frank Norton)

Huntington Avenue, between St. Alphonsus and Worthington Streets, once had impressive apartment buildings that were built when the streetcar tracks were extended in 1882 along Huntington Avenue from the Back Bay. On the far left is the *Harvard*, then the *Carlton* and the *Rutledge* and the *Bartlett* at 660 Huntington Avenue on the far right. The *Harvard* originally had the Harvard Drug Store on the ground floor, and the apartment building is now Smith Hall of Mass Art; the *Carlton* and the *Rutledge* have been demolished and the *Bartlett* is a dormitory for Mass Art.

The *Esther*, on the right, is a Georgian Revival apartment house designed by J. Lawrence Berry, named for owner Esther Brickett and built at Smith Street and Huntington Avenue. On the ground floor was originally the Harvard Branch of the E. F. Mahady medical bookstore as well as a supplier of medical instruments, optical apparatus, photography equipment, and various office supplies. In the foreground, on what had once been row houses at Worthington Street, is a Texaco Service Station. The Texas Fuel Company was founded in Texas in 1901. With its logo of a white star in a red circle was a reference to the lone star of Texas with the adage: "You can trust your car to the man who wears the star." Texaco was the only company selling gasoline under the same brand name in the United States, as well as Canada, making it the most truly national brand among its competitors. It was also one of the Seven Sisters, which dominated the global petroleum industry from the mid-1940s to the 1970s. Today, the Massachusetts College of Pharmacy Griffin Academic Center is on the site of the service station.

The *Helvetia* Apartment Hotel was designed by Robert J. Culbert and built in 1885 at 706-708 Huntington Avenue near Tremont Street. Helvetia is the female national personification of Switzerland, officially *Confoederatio Helvetica*, the Swiss Confederation. When the Queen Anne Revival style four-story brick and brownstone apartment building was built, Huntington Avenue had recently been extended to Brigham Circle three years previously, with electric streetcars servicing the avenue by 1894, and these well-designed buildings, with the corner galvanized iron orioles, created an urban feeling to the streetscape. Notice the Venetian inspired windows on the ground floor set in an arch surmounted by a quatrefoil. (Courtesy of Heidi Adams)

Huntington Avenue, looking east, had by the 1940s become the principal location for medical and educational institutions on the site of the former Ebenezer Francis Estate. Francis was a wealthy merchant and ship owner, one-time treasurer of Harvard College and chairman of the trustees of the Massachusetts General Hospital. To the left of Streetcar 5390 is the Nurses Residence of the Peter Bent Brigham Hospital, in the distance the Martin Grammar School and on the right the *Helvetia* Apartment Hotel.

Fermoyle's Drug Store, at the corner of Huntington Avenue and Tremont Street, was a popular pharmacy and soda fountain. It was a two-story Art Deco inspired red brick and limestone commercial block built in the late 1920s that replaced three wood apartment buildings, the *Neuchatel*, the *Geneva* and the *Lucerne* that were on Tremont Street. Fermoyle's was started in 1946 by Maurice Lurensky, a pharmacist and teacher at New England College of Pharmacy. Later, this was Sawyer Drug Company and Luncheonette. To the left is Jim's Restaurant and the Fenway Manor (apartments). The *Helvita* Apartment building dominates Huntington Avenue, which is lined with wood poles strung with overhead wires for the electric streetcars that connected Brigham Circle with downtown.

Looking West towards Brigham Circle, the intersection of Tremont, Calumet and Francis Streets and Huntington Avenue, the crossroads has long been a busy intersection. Brigham Circle, named for Peter Bent Brigham and located at the intersection of Tremont Street and Huntington Avenue, marks the transition from a residential to medical district and is the main commercial area of Mission Hill. There was once a 12-yard-wide grass circle in the center of the intersection that gave its name to Brigham Circle with wood benches around the edge facing a World War II granite monument with a bronze plaque erected by the Mission Hill Post No. 327 American Legion to the eighty-five men from Mission Hill and Jamaica Plain that gave the supreme sacrifice during the war.

Streetcar 3219 approaches Brigham Circle in 1970, followed by an MBTA bus. The Farragut School can be seen on the left with the Harmon Commercial Block and apartment building. It was designed by Samuel Rantin & Son and built in 1899 as a red brick and sandstone four-unit building with pressed copper bays and a heavily bracketed cornice. There were ground-floor shops including the Circle Delicatessen and Kane's Cleaners and Tailoring shop. Notice the billboard above Kane's, promoting Edward J. Canney, Esq. who was seeking election as a state representative from Wards 10-4; unfortunately, Canney lost to William A. Carey. Today, the Harmon Block has the Brigham and Women's Human Resources Satellite Office, the Laughing Monk Cafe and Penguin.

Streetcar 3028 heads east on Huntington Avenue at Brigham Circle. In the distance is Konner Chevrolet located at 800 Huntington Avenue. Its motto was "More car for your cash—More cash for your car." The new two-story building was completed in 1964 and was touted as "A city block transformed into a masterpiece in glass." Bernard Scher, president, offered the lowest prices ever during Konner's Gigantic Showcase "Showoff Celebration." In the New Showroom with 40,000 square feet of glass were 1964 Chevys ready for immediate delivery, a Used Cars Showroom and a Service Department. To the left is 774, 778 and 782 Huntington Avenue designed by Thomas F. Maguire and built in 1897 of brick with a brick cornice. Today the site on Konner's is the Mission Hill Branch, Massachusetts Eye and Ear and the Brigham & Women's Primary Care Associates.

Streetcar 3037 heads west on Huntington Avenue, having just passed the House of the Good Shepherd, the cupola of which seen in the center. Huntington Avenue was built up in the 1910 to 1920 period with three-story apartment buildings. On the left are 895, 891 and 887 Huntington Avenue. These six family apartment buildings were designed by Silverman Engineering Company and built in 1912 for Morris Weinstein. On the right are 888, 890, 892, 894 and 896 Huntington Avenue designed by J. F. and G. H. Smith and built in 1899 for Davis A. Spivak. Simple in architectural ornamentation, these rows of apartment houses were built of brick and limestone with a now missing galvanized bracketed iron cornice.

Streetcar 6031 heads east on Huntington Avenue, connecting Heath Street in Jamaica Plain with Park Street in Boston. On the left is Konner's Chevrolet, at the corner of Mission Street, with its neon sign and Service Entrance sign. On the right are the Avondale Apartments at 779 Huntington Avenue. On the left, the Avondale Chambers at 777 Huntington Avenue. These two Classical Revival twelve-unit apartment buildings, with Corinthian columned entrances, bracketing, corner quoining and a center pediment, were designed by Jacob Schwartz and built in 1916 of brick and cement for Morris Weinstein. Today St. Albans Street is on the right and Konnor's Chevrolet is now the Massachusetts Eye & Ear and the Brigham & Women's Primary Care Associates.

The impressive apartment building at Huntington Avenue and the Riverway, facing South Huntington Avenue, was designed by Nathaniel Lawrence Silverman and built in 1912. The building was built of brick and limestone in a quasi-Tudor style and once had a heavily bracketed galvanized iron cornice. On the right the Hood delivery truck is stopped at the old Riverside Cafe on the corner. This corner in Mission Hill is one of the busiest in Boston with streetcars turning to the Heath Street Loop and cars going left to Brookline and right to Brigham Circle.

8

BUSINESSES

The Sewell and Day Cordage Company was founded in 1835 by Benjamin Sewall and Moses Day with a ropewalk at the triangular junction of Parker and Ruggles Streets. In 1842, there were nineteen ropewalks in Massachusetts and the longer the ropewalk, the longer was the rope that could be made in one piece. There were a series of ropewalks for different types of cotton rope—small size for fishing lines, mackerel lines and other fine work, spun yarns and other tarred fittings, small hemp rope, 6, 9, and 12 thread as well as hand lead lines, deep sea lines and ordinary manila and cotton clotheslines which were put up in hanks by hand. With Boston's shipbuilding industry and burgeoning mercantile economy, ropemaking was an important part of fitting out a clipper ship, and any improvement in the manufacture of cordage would have given advantage to Boston's overseas traders. The company was acquired by the National Cordage Company in 1891. Today this is part of the campus of Wentworth Institute.

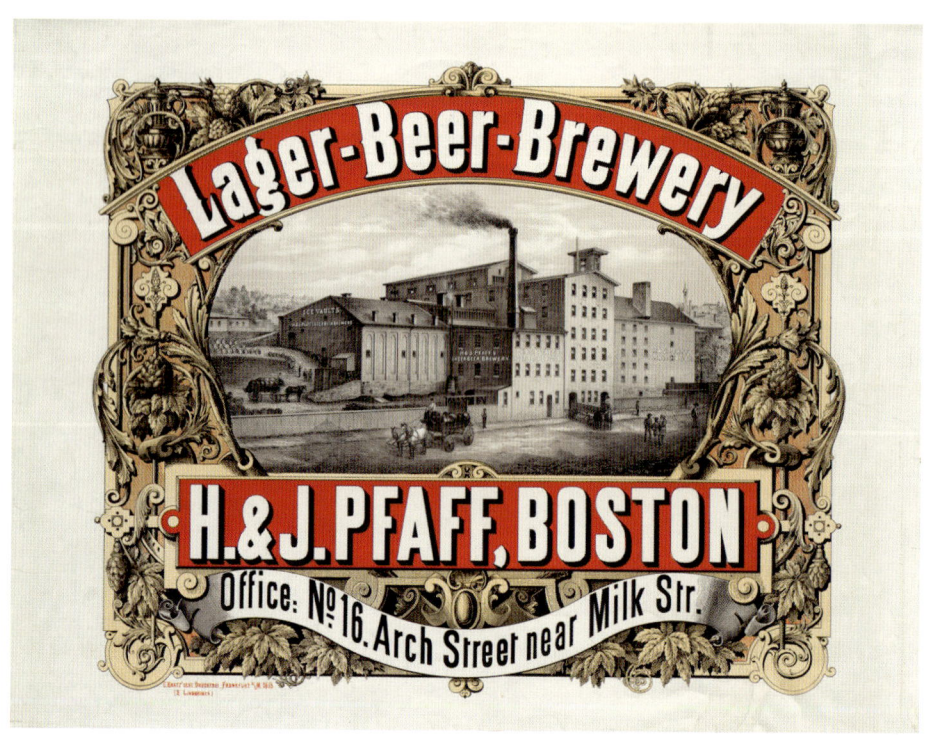

The H. & J. Pfaff Brewery was on Columbus Avenue. Beer has only four ingredients: extract made from malted barley, hops, yeast and water, the latter comprising about 90 percent of the finished product. Pfaff Brewery produced not just beer, but lager. The good, crisp-tasting water of the Stony Brook in Roxbury and Jamaica Plain was crucially important for good beer brewing. Founded in 1857 by brothers Henry and Jacob Pfaff, its beer used the water of the Stony Brook and in 1893 the company became the H. & J. Pfaff Brewing Co. Pfaff survived until Prohibition, which was a nationwide constitutional ban on the production, importation, transportation and sale of alcoholic beverages from 1920 to 1933. Today, the brewery is the present site of Roxbury Community College.

The American Brewing Company was designed by Frederick Footman and built in 1891 at the corner of Heath and Lawn Streets. The American Brewing Company was just one establishment of James W. Kenney, an 1863 Irish immigrant. Kenney also founded the Amory Brewery on Amory Street in 1877, the Park Brewery (Irish ales only) on Terrace Street in 1882 and the Union Brewery (German lager beer only) on Terrace Street in 1893. The ABC Brewing Mill is now repurposed as the American Brewery Lofts. On the building at the corner of Lawn Street, a tall conical metal roof sits atop the tower and once had clocks, which announced the shift hours to the brewery workers.

The Highland Spring Brewery was designed by J. Williams Beal and built at 166 Terrace Street. From 1867 to 1885, wonderful processes ruled this brewery, which had a little arched refrigeration building, the first for a brewery in this country, and a bottling building. The name changed to Rueter & Company, which operated as the largest ale and pottery brewery until Prohibition closed its doors in 1919. It later became a warehouse for the Oliver Ditson Company, a noted music publisher. After Prohibition Croft Brewing Company made Croft Ale there from 1934 to 1953 and one building was converted into the Rosoff Pickle factory. The brewery-cum-pickle factory was repurposed recently as the Oliver Lofts.

The Roxbury Buick Dealership was at 590 Huntington Avenue and sold cars manufactured by the car company founded by David Dunbar Buick. Its sleek modern plate glass and chrome showroom had the latest Buicks in 1950, but they also offered used cars. The 1950 Buick Roadmaster Convertible was the top of the line for Buick and their advertisement said: "You're Lord of Every Highway in the Luxurious Roadmaster." In 1950 one might also choose a Buick Roadmaster Riviera Estate Wagon, a Roadmaster Estate Wagon, a Roadmaster Jetback Sedanet or a Roadmaster Deluxe Riviera. After World War II with the ascendancy of the automobile, the ease of travel on the federally funded and built interstate highway system boosted auto sales. Today this is a park at Wentworth Institute, at the corner of Vancouver Street.

Jim's Restaurant was on Huntington Avenue near Tremont Street. It was a longtime favorite place to get traditional cooking by both local residents and medical workers. It was owned by James Bournazos; as his grandson, Robert Poulos, recalled, "The food was diner type, comfort food. Good quality for a fair price." Notice the sign in the window offering breakfast. In addition, the daily specials included spaghetti and meatballs and meatloaf and liver and onions. Bread pudding was a favorite dessert. Every Friday night a fish dinner was on the menu, a New England tradition, and was served by longtime waitress, Dotty Newhall.

Travers Tavern was established in 1897 by Jim Travers at 134 Smith Street, at the corner of Worthington Street. It was a popular neighborhood pub with neighborhood regulars but also students from nearby Wentworth Institute and Mass College of Art. Owned by Thomas English since 1966, it was one of many bars he and later his family owned and operated throughout the city of Boston including Dorchester, West Roxbury, Hyde Park, Mattapan, Mission Hill and South Boston, as well as Quincy and Cambridge. The tavern, with a mock Tudor exterior, was operated by the English Family, the second owners, until 1996. The pub later became the Squealing Pig. The advertised drink on the signboard is Chimay Peres Trappistes, a highly fermented Trappist beer with a touch of hops and spicy aromas that never fails to delight all who taste it. (Courtesy of Mary Ann English)

Though not a business per se, the Parker Hill Branch of the Boston Public Library offers community residents everything from books, newspapers, magazines, lectures and children's activities, as well as social networking. The library first opened a reading room and book drop at 1518 Tremont Street in 1907; the present Gothic Revival stone library was designed by Ralph Adams Cram, built in 1931 and has the seal of the Boston Public Library above the front door. In front of the library is Dolly's Garden, a tribute to Dolly DeSimone, the Children's Librarian at the branch for more than twenty years.

9

URBAN RENEWAL

Though much of Mission Hill's housing was built in the 1880 to 1925 period and included a panoply of architectural styles and various sized housing units, the area along St. Alphonsus Street to Ward Street was declared a blighted area by the city of Boston in the late 1930s. The Boston Redevelopment Authority, with funding from the Federal Works Agency United States Housing Authority, undertook an urban renewal project with a low-rent housing development on the eastern slope of Mission Hill. This huge sign at Ward and Parker Streets proclaims that there will be a low-rent housing project on Mission Hill, with the twin towers and lantern of the Basilica of Our Lady of Perpetual Help rising in the distance, which offered a sense of continuity.

The Bridget Egan House was built in the late 1860s at 176 Ward Street at the corner of St. Alphonsus Street and would be demolished, along with much of the surrounding neighborhood, in the late 1930s to make was for the Mission Hill Housing Development. The domestic scale of the nineteenth-century architecture was swept away with new three-story red brick buildings that were aligned in regimented rows without through streets, and with very little parking except on the street. On the right is the rear of the *Harvard* Apartment Building at 640-644 Huntington Avenue.

In 1961, wholesale demolition of numerous properties on Mission Hill was taking place along Tremont Street and St. Alphonsus Street to make way for a modern twenty-four-story apartment building. White's Market was on the ground floor of this three-decker at the corner of Tremont and St. Alphonsus Streets and was one of 116 buildings demolished with the approval of the Boston Redevelopment Authority; to the left rear of White's can be seen the Our Lady of Perpetual Help Grammar School in background. Houses located on Conant, Whitney, Worthington, St. Alphonsus and Tremont Streets were swept away in the name of a second wave of urban renewal. Today the Longwood Apartments is on the site.

The Boston Housing Authority, established by Mayor Frederick Mansfield and the Boston City Council in 1935, built the Mission Hill Housing Development in 1940 under a federal program that provided low-cost public housing. These were brand new three-story buildings arranged in neat and tidy rows, and maintenance responded to problems. It was said in 1941 to be "a nice and sociable place to live in with plenty of children who played together in the streets. The houses were compact, but handy and easy to clean." The Mission Hill Housing Development was among the first housing project opened in the United States. Seen here, looking east on St. Alphonsus Street in 1947, it was a model for urban redevelopment. Redeveloped in 2002, it is now known as Mission Main and has 545 mixed income units. On the left is now Cityview at Longwood.

The Charlesbank Cooperative, a twenty-four-story apartment building, was designed by Hugh Stubbins Associates and built in 1963 at 650 Huntington Avenue on recently cleared land on Mission Hill. Demolition cranes can still be seen on the left on St. Alphonsus Street with the cupola and twin spires and lantern of the Mission Church rising in the distance. When completed, the International Style high-rise building had one tier of balconies located off-center on each of the four facades, giving the tower a pinwheel shape. Today, the Charlesbank is a 276-unit high-rise that became a limited equity co-operative, and after one year of rental, residents own shares in the building but do not own their apartment.

Seen looking east from the top of Parker Hill is what is now known as the Kevin W. Fitzgerald Park, formerly Puddingstone Park. The Park was constructed by the One Brigham Circle development project and funded by the Edward Ingersoll Browne Trust and One Brigham Circle LLC. The Park is owned by Friends of Puddingstone Park and was renamed in 2006 after Fitzgerald, who was a state representative, Sergeant at Arms in the Massachusetts State House and co-founder of the Center for the Study of Sport in Society at Northeastern University. The overlay of architecture from the nineteenth century to the present is evident with the Basilica of Our Lady of Perpetual Help, the Rectory and the Longwood Apartments, designed by William R. Hooper of Hooper & Sirkis Engineers and built in 1964 at 1575 Tremont Street. The panoramic view from this urban hilltop park offers a unique perspective to downtown Boston, the city that annexed Roxbury in 1868.